JUN 0 1 2017

Exceptional
Asians

BRENDA SONG

*Actress
and
Singer*

Portia Summers

E **Enslow Publishing**
101 W. 23rd Street
Suite 240
New York, NY 10011
USA

enslow.com

Words to Know

charity—Help given to people in need.

heiress—A woman who will inherit a lot of money or property.

Hmong—A group of people living in Asia, specifically certain areas of China, Vietnam, Laos, and Thailand.

recurring role—A character on a show that continues to reappear over time.

reincarnation—Someone who has died and been brought back to life.

spin-off—A television show that is based on the characters first introduced in another show.

stunt—An action done in a film or show that requires athletic skill.

taekwondo—A Korean martial art with an emphasis on kicks.

voiceover—Narration over a film or television show where the speaker is not seen.

Contents

Brenda Song

CHAPTER 1

A Star Is Born

Brenda Julietta Song was born on March 27, 1988, in Carmichael, California. Her father is **Hmong**, which is a group from China and Vietnam. Her mother is Thai. The couple were both born in Asia but met in Sacramento, California, as adults.

Brenda is the eldest of three children. She has two younger brothers, Timmy and Nathan. As a child, Brenda was spotted in a San Francisco mall by a talent agent, who got Brenda work as a child model. She began appearing in commercials when she was five years old, including commercials for Little Caesars Pizza and Barbie.

At six years old, Brenda and her mother moved to Los Angeles to pursue her acting career. Her father and brothers followed two years later.

An Important Hobby

When she was young, Brenda wanted to take ballet. Her brothers wanted to take **taekwondo**. Because Brenda's mother didn't want to have to take her children to two different activities, Brenda began taking taekwondo classes with her brothers. At the time, she hated it. However, it would be very helpful later in her career.

As a child, Brenda took taekwondo classes with her brothers.

Brenda Says:

"I was just a little girl watching TV and wanting to be in it. My parents had no idea how to get me there, but here I am as a part of this great cast on the Disney Channel. Truly, if you just want to do this, then you have to commit to it."

A Young Actress

In 1995, when she was seven years old, Brenda landed her first big acting role, in the film *Requiem*. Soon, she was regularly going to auditions and working on TV shows and movies. Over the next few years she earned several TV and movie roles. But it was not until 2000 that Brenda's career really began to take off.

CHAPTER 2

Disney

In 2000, Brenda was cast in the Disney Channel movie *The Ultimate Christmas Present*. Brenda starred as one of the girls who discovers a weather machine and makes it snow in Los Angeles for Christmas. For her portrayal of Samantha Kwan, Brenda received a Young Artist Award.

Bigger and Better Roles

In 2002, Brenda guest-starred on *The Bernie Mac Show*. She was awarded another Young Artist Award. And that was only the beginning of a big

Brenda poses with Hallee Hirsh, her co-star in *The Ultimate Christmas Present.*

year for Brenda. She also starred in the big-screen film *Like Mike* alongside rapper Lil' Bow Wow. But perhaps the biggest event that occurred that year was her contract with Disney. It meant she was promised more work with the famous children's television channel.

Because she was so busy with work, Brenda never went to a regular school. She was homeschooled. Brenda loved to read and study. When she was in the ninth grade she received an All-American Scholar Award for academic excellence. She earned her high school diploma at sixteen, but she didn't want to stop learning. She took online classes from the University of California at Berkeley, studying psychology and business.

Brenda Says:

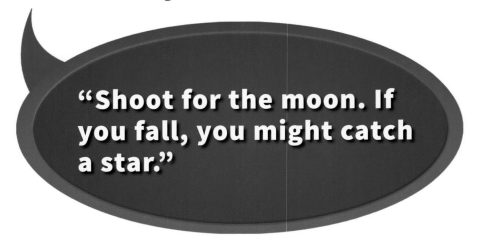

"Shoot for the moon. If you fall, you might catch a star."

Brenda, third from right, performs in a scene from the 2002 movie *Like Mike*.

Between 2003 and 2004, Brenda made many appearances on Disney Channel shows, including *That's So Raven* and *Phil of the Future*. In 2004, she starred in another Disney Channel movie, *Stuck in the Suburbs*. It was during this time that she began to be recognized widely by audiences. It was an exciting time for Brenda. Her career was really taking off.

CHAPTER 3

The *Suite Life* of Brenda

In 2005, Brenda landed the role of her career. The Disney Channel was casting for a new television show that took place in a fancy hotel in Boston. Even though she didn't audition, Brenda was offered the role of the hotel **heiress**. She took it.

Ditzy, wealthy London Tipton had a huge closet filled with designer clothes and shoes, and she didn't seem to understand the troubles of people who weren't wealthy. But Brenda loved playing her. Brenda says that London's personality was not like hers, but sometimes it felt like it was a part of her.

Brenda hangs out with her *Suite Life* co-stars, Dylan Sprouse (left) and his brother, Cole.

Success

On March 18, 2005, *The Suite Life of Zack and Cody* premiered on the Disney Channel. It was a hit! Audiences loved London's bubbly personality and her outlook on life. Before long, she was appearing more and more in each episode.

The *Suite Life of Zack and Cody* was so popular that it inspired a **spin-off** in 2008: *The Suite Life on*

Deck. From 2008 to 2011, the *Suite Life* characters became the longest-running continuous characters in Disney history. Brenda played the channel's longest-running female character.

More Than an Actress

But Brenda didn't stop there. She began doing **voiceover** work on another Disney Channel show: *American Dragon, Jake Long*. She also provided the voice of Trick in the animated movie *Holidaze: The Christmas That Almost Didn't Happen*.

Brenda Says:

"To this day, just always treat people the way you want to be treated. . . . Whether you have success or don't have it, whether you're a good person is all that matters."

In the Disney TV movie *Wendy Wu: Homecoming Warrior*, Brenda plays an average teen who must learn martial arts in order to save the world.

Wendy Wu

In 2006, the Disney Channel was casting a made-for-TV movie about a Chinese-American girl who is the **reincarnation** of a warrior. They wanted someone who was young and funny and knew about martial arts. Brenda was perfect for the role. *Wendy Wu: Homecoming Warrior* became a big hit. In the movie, Brenda did all her own **stunts**, since she has a black belt in taekwondo.

A New Kind of Role

In 2010, Brenda appeared in *The Social Network*, a film about Mark Zuckerberg, the inventor of Facebook. It was a big-budget movie for an adult audience. Brenda now had the chance to show her more serious side. She was growing up, and it was time for her to take her career in new directions.

Brenda appears in a scene from *The Social Network* with co-stars Jesse Eisenberg (left) and Andrew Garfield.

CHAPTER 4

All Grown Up

By 2011, when *The Suite Life on Deck* ended, Brenda was getting too old to be a Disney star. She was now twenty-three. Most of the stars on the Disney Channel are kids. Brenda was ready to branch out and use her fame to draw attention to causes important to her.

Brenda's Causes

Brenda has been working with **charities** since she became famous. She was the hostess of the 2006 "A World Of Change" fashion show, where all the money made helped the Optimist Youth Homes and Family

Services organization. Brenda also speaks about breast cancer awareness, a cause that is dear to her because her mother is a breast cancer survivor.

Brenda believes that healthy eating and living are important. She brought awareness to the

Brenda attends a 2013 benefit for women's cancer.

Brenda Says:

"Your body is like a machine, and if you don't keep it in shape, it holds you back. You don't want anything holding you back, especially yourself."

importance of a healthy diet in Disney's "Pass the Plate" campaign. Here, she helped families learn about healthy food and exercise.

After Disney

Even though she has stopped working for Disney, Brenda hasn't stopped acting. She has had many **recurring** roles in television shows, including *Scandal* and *New Girl*. She also had a starring role in Fox's *Dads*, but the sitcom was cancelled in 2014 after one season.

Brenda calls herself a dork. She loves reading and writing in her journal. She'd rather stay at home and watch movies than go to a big party. She is also an avid LA Lakers fan and can often be seen cheering them on at games.

Brenda is close with her family and proud of her heritage. She celebrates Hmong New Year in her hometown of Carmichael, California, every year.

For a multi-talented young woman like Brenda Song, stardom has just begun. Fans can certainly look forward to seeing her in more TV, film, and music roles, as well as charity events and educational programs. Brenda will surely continue to be in the spotlight for many years to come.

Brenda has said that she wants to be a role model for young people. She encourages them to follow their dreams, just as she has.

Timeline

1988—Brenda Julietta Song is born in Carmichael, California.

1993—Begins modeling and acting in commercials.

1994—Moves to Los Angeles to pursue her acting career.

1995—Gets a role in *Requiem* at age seven.

1999—Appears in *Once and Again* and *Popular*.

2000—Stars in *The Ultimate Christmas Present*; receives a Young Artist Award.

2002—Signs contract with Disney.

2005—Stars as London Tipton in *The Suite Life of Zack and Cody*.

2006—Stars in *Wendy Wu: Homecoming Warrior*; hosts "A World of Change" charity event.

2009—Appears on *The Social Network*.

2012—Stars in *First Kiss* and has a recurring role on *Scandal*.

2013—Begins recurring role on *New Girl*; stars in *Dads*.

2015—Provides voiceover for *Miles From Tomorrowland*; stars in *Take It From Us*.

Learn More

Books

Kingston, Anna. *Respecting the Contributions of Asian Americans*. New York: PowerKids Press, 2012.

Mayfield, Katherine. *Acting A to Z: The Young Person's Guide to a Stage or Screen Career*. New York: Back Stage Books, 2010.

Orr, Tamra. *Brenda Song*. Hockessin, DE: Mitchell Lane Publishers, 2009.

Websites

tv.com/people/brenda-song-1/
Photos, trivia, and news about Brenda Song.

disneychannel.disney.com/the-suite-life-of-zack-and-cody
Official site of *The Suite Life of Zack and Cody*.

Index

Published in 2017 by Enslow Publishing, LLC.
101 W. 23rd Street, Suite 240, New York, NY 10011

Copyright © 2017 by Enslow Publishing, LLC.
All rights reserved.

No part of this book may be reproduced by any means without the written permission of the publisher.

Library of Congress Cataloging-in-Publication Data
Names: Summers, Portia, author.
Title: Brenda Song : actress and singer / Portia Summers.
Description: New York : Enslow Publishing, 2017. | Series: Exceptional Asians | Includes bibliographical references and index.
Identifiers: LCCN 2015047176| ISBN 9780766078406 (library bound) | ISBN 9780766078468 (pbk.) | ISBN 9780766078079 (6-pack)
Subjects: LCSH: Song, Brenda, 1988---Juvenile literature. | Actors--United States--Biography--Juvenile literature. | Singers--United States--Biography--Juvenile literature. | Asian American actresses--United States--Biography--Juvenile literature.
Classification: LCC PN2287.S635 S86 2017 | DDC 791.4302/8092--dc23
LC record available at http://lccn.loc.gov/2015047176

Printed in Malaysia

To Our Readers: We have done our best to make sure all website addresses in this book were active and appropriate when we went to press. However, the author and the publisher have no control over and assume no liability for the material available on those websites or on any websites they may link to. Any comments or suggestions can be sent by e-mail to customerservice@enslow.com.

Photo Credits: Throughout book, ©Toria/Shutterstock.com (blue background); cover, p. 1 Helga Esteb/Shutterstock.com; p. 4 Alberto E. Rodriguez/Getty Images; p. 6 Kzenon/Shutterstock.com; pp. 9, 15, 16 AF archive/Alamy Stock Photo; p. 11 ZUMA Press Inc/Alamy Stock Photo; p. 13 Gary Gershoff/WireImage/Getty Images; p. 18 Imeh Akpanudosen/Getty Images for FIJI Water; p. 21 GUNN FILMS WALT DISNEY PICTURES WETCHER, BARRY/Album/Newscom.